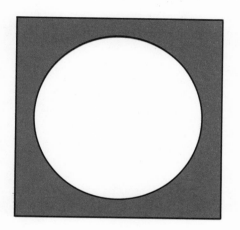

THE LIBERATOR
(ELEUTHERIOS)

THE
LIBERATOR
(ELEUTHERIOS)

by Da Free John

THE DAWN HORSE PRESS
CLEARLAKE, CALIFORNIA

4/95

Printed in the United States of America
International Standard Book Number:
Cloth 0-913922-66-8
Paper 0-913922-67-6

Produced by The Johannine Daist Communion in cooperation with
The Dawn Horse Press

THE JOHANNINE DAIST COMMUNION

CONTENTS

INTRODUCTION

The
Gift of
Liberation

Our world is teeming with millions of ordinary destinies, caught in bewilderment and suffering. Today, when the threat of global annihilation casts its spell on our lives, uncertainty, doubt, fear, and universal foolishness are more prevalent than ever before in the history of mankind. It is in critical periods such as ours that the Divine Being manifests Itself in the form of a destiny that is in every respect extraordinary and remarkable. Thus, because the Divine life of Master Da Free John is not at all part of the chain of deluded human existence, it carries the force to change the very course of human history.

Master Da Free John is one of those rare beings who incarnate into the earthly plane of existence already Illumined, and who are born with the exceptional capacity for rapid personal evolution for the sake of the spiritual Enlightenment of mankind. Master Da's early life was itself a manifestation of the lesson he has come to Teach mankind about the fruitlessness of seeking. His first thirty years were a trial of spiritual aspiration or a sacred ordeal that prepared him for his future Mission. His early life bears out that he was fated to fulfill the destiny of a spiritual giant who could conquer the complacency and ignorance that are oppressing all of mankind.

I *was born on the basis of the impulse to bring the Living Divine Reality into the human plane and to Teach its Realization. Beyond this human plane, God is already Realized in my case. My impulse was to accept the conditions of embodiment and to Realize the Divine in the human plane.*

The purpose of my life is, through struggle, to bring the Divine Reality into life in human form, to communicate Its Argument and Its Way, and to Transmit It directly through the Power of Spiritual Revelation. This process of Transmission is made available to devotees who come directly into my physical company on the basis of the Teaching. Such devotees are then the principal individuals to be granted this Revelation in the course of their practice. But my Spiritual Blessing and Awakening Power are granted universally throughout all space-time and therefore to the entire world and the cosmos.

Master Da was born Enlightened (or Awake in the Transcendental Condition of self and Nature) on the third of November, 1939, into an unsuspecting middle-class family of the Long Island suburbs of New York City and into a crassly materialistic culture. From the time of his birth the spiritual process was already fully active in him. As a growing child Franklin Jones, as he was named, underwent a profound physical and psychic purification, enduring "inexplicable" physical symptoms such as high fevers, which were diagnosed as signs of disease. Within his first seven years he passed through a profusion of mystical phenomena such as visions, dramatic psychic revelations, and states of devotional ecstasy. By the time he had matured through adolescence, he had become acutely frustrated with the social and religious conventions of Western society.

At the age of seventeen he left his home, thereby frustrating the hopes and expectations of his family and friends that he would live out an ordinary destiny. His renunciation, like his birth, was a sacrifice for the sake of the spiritual perfection of others. He freely renounced all possible worldly and conventional religious ambitions. But instead of seeking out the quietude of a remote cave or forest, he entered the jungle of twentieth-century America.

Shortly after leaving home, "Franklin Jones" underwent a major transformation in consciousness.

Quite *suddenly, in a moment, I experienced a total revolution of energy and awareness in myself. An absolute sense of understanding opened and arose at the extreme end of all this consciousness. And I felt a surge of force draw up out of my depths and expand, filling my whole body and every level of my consciousness with wave on wave of the most beautiful and joyous energy.*

I felt absolutely mad, but the madness was not of a desperate kind. There was no seeking and no dilemma within it, no question, no unfulfilled motive, not a single object or presence outside myself.

(The Knee of Listening)

Subsequently a whole succession of teachers (including humans, animals, discarnate beings, and natural forces) as well as extraordinary experiences and unusual powers entered the orbit of his life. He dedicated himself to them with the utmost intensity, quickly assimilating and mastering the teachings and disciplines given to him at the various stages of his spiritual development. He always entered into a fully committed relationship with his teachers, but each encounter was a test of his capacity to understand and transcend every lesson and attainment in the Light of his prior Illumination. When their intrinsic limitations as embodiments of seeking had become obvious to him, he did not merely abandon his teachers or disciplines. Nor did he attempt to forcedly integrate what he had learned. Rather, he transcended all of them, and the force of his prior Enlightenment revealed to him the futility of seeking as he moved beyond the traditional paths.

The uniqueness of Master Da's life lies in the fact that the Divine Being, Mind, and Power has Itself been his Teacher or Master, not any secondary influence, earthly or cosmic. Thus, in the course of Master Da's life a new Revelation of the Divine Reality has emerged to purify and transform the traditions of seeking and to turn mankind to the Truth. His life is the dramatic story of the breakthrough of the Radiant Being, of Divine Consciousness, into the human world. Master Da gives this ecstatic testimony:

But always the Divine Self or very God has been my Teacher. The Living God is my Teacher. I am the servant of the Living God. The Form of the Great One is manifested fully in me. I am the living agent of the Divine

Person, the Transcendental Being, Who is always, already, and universally Present, and Who does not incarnate separately. That One is Revealed through agents, who, by virtue of perfect non-obstruction, manifest the Divine Person, the Self of all, perfectly. But they point to the Transcendental Being as Eternal God, Master, and very Self. This is my Work, and it is only now about to begin. I was born for this. The Transforming Work is complete.

This transforming Work was fully accomplished when, at thirty years of age, his spiritual quest came to an end in one of the most momentous spiritual events ever recorded. At the Vedanta Temple in Los Angeles, California, he Realized the very Source and Ultimate Goal of all the traditions of seeking.

A*s time passed there was no sensation, no movement at all. There was not even any kind of deepening. There was no meditation. There was no need for meditation. There was not a single element to be added to my consciousness. I sat with my eyes open. I was not having an experience of any kind.*

In an instant, I became profoundly and directly aware of what I am. It was a tacit realization, a direct knowledge in consciousness itself. It was consciousness itself without the addition of a communication from any other source. I simply sat there and knew what I am. I was being what I am. I am Reality, the Self, and Nature and Support of all things and all beings. I am the One Being, known as God, the One Mind, the Self.

There was no thought involved in this. I am that Consciousness. There was no reaction of either joy or surprise. I am the One I recognized. I am that One. I am not merely experiencing Him.

Then truly there was no more to realize. Every experience in my life had led to this. My entire life had been the communication of that Reality to me, until I am That.
(The Knee of Listening)

The One of which Master Da speaks is the Transcendental Truth or Source-Consciousness of the world and every being. The demand for the Realization of that Divine Truth is placed on every single person by the Divine Being, to Whom Master Da refers by the Name "Da" (meaning "the One Who Gives Freely to all") and the Title "Eleutherios," which means "the Liberator." Eleutherios, which Title was bestowed on the Supreme Deity in ancient Greece, is also Master Da Free John, who is Free in the Truth. His Liberating Message is the Grace that can transform the life of anyone who enters wholeheartedly into his Truthful Company.

The true Way is the one that is blissful now. The true Teaching turns you to present bliss and does not require you to create it. All ways that turn you to paths, goals, gradual attainments, and the idea of a necessary and ultimate future that is an evolutionary and revolutionary

15

state unknown in the present are false. They are pat-
terned after the model of separation and are only forms
of seeking. Understanding is present bliss, unqualified
freedom and Reality, Consciousness Itself without motion
or necessity.

(The Knee of Listening)

The Realization of Transcendental Consciousness, or Divine Truth and Happiness and Freedom, is the quintessence of Master Da's Teaching. He is alive not merely to be an example of proper social attitudes and behaviors, but to Liberate living beings from the conventional bondage to the body-mind and its world of finite relations. This book is Master Da's compassionate offering to a self-enslaved mankind; he brings the Gift of Liberation in Truth.

Georg Feuerstein
The Mountain of Attention
July 4, 1982

ΕΛΕΥΘΕΡΙΟΣ

PROLOGUE

When the Body
Is Full
of Light

Mindless embodiment.
Consciousness without inwardness.
Thus It becomes Obvious.

Every object is only Light, the Energy of
Consciousness.
Even so, there is no mind.
Only this stark embodiment, without inwardness.

First transcend the mind, not the body.
Inwardness is flight from Life and Love.
Only the body is Full of Consciousness.

Therefore, be the body-only, feeling into Life.
Surrender the mind into Love, until the body
dissolves in Light.
Dare this Ecstasy, and never be made thoughtful by
birth and experience and death.

I

Eleutherios

Truth is the ultimate form (or state) of knowledge.

Truth is That which, when known (or fully Realized), sets you free from all bondage and all seeking.

Truth is Eleutherios, the Liberator.

God is not the awful Creator, the world-making and ego-making Titan, the Nature-God of worldly theology. God is not the First Cause, the Other, or any of the Objective Ideas of mind-made philosophy. God is not any Image created by the religious ego. God is not any Power contacted by the mystical or the scientific ego. God is not any Goal that motivates the social ego.

God is Truth, or That which, when known (or fully Realized), sets you entirely free.

God is Eleutherios, the Liberator.

THREE

God is not, in Truth, the Cause or the Objective Origin of the world and the ego (or separate self-consciousness). All causes (including any Ultimate Objective Cause) are only conditional modifications of Objective Nature.

Every cause is moving energy, or the conditional mover of energy. Therefore, the Ultimate Cause is, in Itself, only Energy, or the Conditional Mover of Energy. No cause, and no Cause of causes, is Truth Itself, since to know a cause (or the Cause) is merely to know an object (or the Object) and not to be liberated from bondage to the search for objective existence itself.

The knowledge of objects does not set you free, since it is the knower (rather than the known) that knows itself to be bound. Freedom can only be Realized by transcending the subject (or knower) of knowledge, not by increasing the objects of knowledge. Therefore, freedom is not Realized even in the attainment of an Ultimate Object of knowledge.

FOUR

God is not the Cause, or the Objective Origin of the world. God is the Source, or the Subjective Origin of the world. The Cause of causes is not Truth, since to know such a Cause does not set you free. Therefore, if you are to be free, the Subjective Source of that Cause (and of all causes) must be known.

The existence of God is not proven (or even made perfectly convincing) by appeal to the process of objective causation. But the existence of God is Self-Evident in the consideration of the Subjective Source of all causes, all effects, all seeking, all knowledge, and the self-consciousness that engages in causes, effects, seeking, and knowledge.

FIVE

God is Consciousness, or the Subjective Source of the world and the self. The Deep Space of Consciousness is the Matrix in which the Origin and Condition of self, mind, body, world, the entire cosmos of Nature, and the Universal Field of Energy is inherently Obvious. When this is known (or when Consciousness is fully Realized), the world and the self are fully known (and thus transcended) in Truth. To know God as Consciousness, or the Subjective Source of the world and the self, is to transcend both the world and the self by means of Truth, or the only knowledge that can set you free.

God is not known by the body (or in the process of bodily experience), since God is not reducible to any kind of object (or Objective Force).

God confronts you bodily, materially, or in the objective plane of Nature only in the form of effects (or an Effective Influence). Therefore, God cannot be known as God (or Truth) via any confrontation in the objective realm of Nature. Objective effects (including an Ultimate Objective Influence) are only conditional or representative forms of God. Therefore, bodily experience, or bodily confrontation with Objective Nature, does not prove or even necessarily indicate or point to the existence of God.

No bodily experience is an encounter with Truth.

No bodily experience can set you free.

God is not an Object or Image or Idea that can confront the mind. Whatever confronts (or is known by) the mind only modifies and occupies the mind itself. Occupation with ideas, or states of mind, can only motivate you toward further activities of mind and body. Therefore, there is no Idea that is Truth, since attention to an Idea cannot liberate attention from mind itself.

EIGHT

Bodily experience and mental knowledge are both based on encounters with objects. In general, bodily experience and mental knowledge motivate you to seek more bodily experience and more mental knowledge. Your seeking, therefore, is for more and more encounters with bodily and mental objects.

Your <u>search</u> for bodily and mental objects is your bondage. It is the sign of a fundamental stress, or presumed unhappiness. If you understand that your search is unhappiness, then you stand free in relation to all of your possible objects, all of your possible experiences, and all of your possible ideas. This understanding transcends experiences and ideas. It reduces your motivation toward objects, and thus it permits your attention to contemplate the otherwise uninspected Subjective Source that is God, Truth, or the Liberator, Eleutherios.

NINE

God, Truth, Reality, or Happiness cannot be Found, Located, or Realized by the movement of attention in the midst of the objects, relations, conditions, or states of the individual (or experientially defined) self.

God, Truth, Reality, or Happiness cannot be Found or Attained by the movement of attention in the Objective realm of Nature, or what is not recognized to be Consciousness.

God, Truth, Reality, or Happiness cannot be Located by the ego within the egoic body-mind.

God, Truth, Reality, or Happiness is not reducible to Objective Energy, or any subjective or objective form of the Energy that seems to pervade all of Nature and to be the Ultimate Object of individuated consciousness and experience.

All seeking finally leads to the consideration of Consciousness and profound Identification with Consciousness Itself.

Consciousness, which is Self-Radiant, Uncaused, Unchanging, Transcendental Being, and Eternal Love-Bliss, is God, Truth, Reality, and Happiness.

Therefore, God, Truth, Reality, or Happiness is Located and Realized by transcending the bondage of attention to the conditional self (or body-mind) and its relations.

This is done only by returning attention to Intuitive Identification with its Source-Condition, or the Self-Radiant Domain of Blissful Consciousness.

ELEVEN

Consciousness is the ultimate form (or state) of knowledge.

The Realization of perfect Identification with Consciousness, which is the Subjective Source (rather than the Object) of experience and knowledge, is better described as Ignorance, rather than knowledge, since it transcends all objective and conventionally subjective categories of experience and knowledge.

Consciousness is That which, when fully Realized, sets you free from all bondage and all seeking.

Consciousness is God.

Consciousness is the Truth.

Consciousness is the Liberator, Eleutherios.

TWELVE

All objects are only apparent relations of Consciousness.

Objects appear to Consciousness when It consents to be active as attention in relation to a body-mind in the conditional realm of Nature.

Consciousness Itself is never separate, limited, individual, conditional, or unhappy.

Consciousness is the Transcendental, One, and Eternal Principle of existence.

When viewed by the Transcendental Consciousness, all objects are inherently recognizable as the Happiness or Radiant Love-Bliss of Transcendental Being.

There are, in Truth, no objects, but there is only Radiant Transcendental Being, Consciousness, or Happiness.

When everything is Realized to be Consciousness, there is only Consciousness.

Then there is only Truth, or freedom from all bondage to self and world.

Then you are Eleutherios, Consciousness, the Truth, or Freedom Itself.

Be Consciousness.

Contemplate Consciousness.

Transcend everything in Consciousness.

This is the Epitome of the Way of Truth.

The necessary instrument for the Realization of Transcendental Consciousness is free attention. Therefore, as a base for that Realization, you must establish the body-mind in a stable condition of equanimity (wherein attention is naturally free). To do so, listen to the radical Argument of the Adept Spiritual Master until there is true "hearing," in the form of profound consideration, understanding, easy self-discipline, and spontaneous feeling-surrender of self.

When attention is thus set free from binding attachment to the conditions of the body-mind, it is free to invert upon the Subjective Source in which self and world are transparent to Bliss. And the Ultimate Event of Transcendental Awakening is then Served by "seeing," or devotional surrender into the Mindless Company, Radiant Presence, and Supreme Grace of Transmission that are Offered freely by the Adept Spiritual Master.

This is the Liberating Truth, the Great Message that I bring to you from the Divine Domain.

II

What
Is
Consciousness?

ONE

Consider this.

From the point of view of the individuated self there are apparently two principles in manifestation. There is individual consciousness (or attention, the witness of objects), and there is everything else (or the possible objects of that consciousness).

You exist as consciousness, and as consciousness you experience many kinds of objects (or relations and states of consciousness). You tend merely to experience (rather than to consider and transcend) those objects, relations, and states, and so you develop a sense of identification with some, a desire for some others, and a revulsion toward certain others.

This complex of identification, desire, and aversion is the summary of your conventional existence. And in the midst of all of that you are afraid, bewildered, and constantly moved to achieve some kind of experience or knowledge that will enable you to feel utterly released, free, and happy.

In fact, you never achieve ultimate experience, knowledge, release, freedom, or happiness. And so your existence is a constant search for these, while you are otherwise bound to fear, bewilderment, self-possession, desire, and aversion.

There is a perfect alternative to this bondage and seeking. It is not a matter of the egoic attainment of any object, knowledge, or state of psycho-physical fulfillment or release. Rather, it is a matter of entering into an <u>alternative view</u> of experience. Instead of <u>merely</u> experiencing (and so developing the qualities of identification, desire, aversion, fear, bewilderment, and the search for knowledge, release, freedom, fulfillment, and happiness), inspect and consider your own condition and, from that point of view, examine and consider all of your experience.

If you inspect and consider your own condition and all of your experience, rather than merely submit to experience, it should become clear that you are consciousness, and all of the objects or varieties of experience appear to you <u>only</u> as a play upon (or modification of) consciousness. Experience (or the modification and limitation of consciousness) is not the dominant factor of your existence. Consciousness is the dominant and always prior factor, but you tend always (by virtue of a mechanical involvement with experience) to be submitted to and controlled by experience. Because of this mechanical involvement with experience, you constantly forget and abandon your basic position, and you suffer the disturbances I have already described.

TWO

The basic qualification for the most direct consideration of existence is the capacity to stand as stably free attention (able to constantly inspect and consider the conditions of existence rather than merely to be controlled by experience). On the basis of that free attention, you can directly inspect and consider your actual condition in relation to <u>all</u> experience. If this is done, it is obvious that you are simply consciousness (whatever that <u>is</u> ultimately). You are always already established in that standpoint. You always already exist <u>as</u> that very consciousness, rather than as the presumption of identification with the body-mind—which presumption is a convention of the body-mind, or a sense of identity that is superimposed on consciousness subsequent to the mechanical arising of experience. If you inspect and consider experience in every moment from the native standpoint of consciousness, it is evident that whatever is arising is always arising to (or, really, within) consciousness and as an apparent modification of consciousness. Your original or native position is consciousness, and if consciousness will consider experience from the point of view of consciousness, rather than first submit itself to be controlled by experience and known only subsequently and from the point of view of experience, then consciousness is already established in its own natural or native standpoint, directly and freely aware that it is being confronted and modified or played upon in the evident form of various kinds of objects or superimpositions. By abiding continually in this native standpoint relative to experience, you become more and more profoundly aware of and as consciousness itself (rather than more and more mechanically aware of the objects, experiences, and states of conditional identity that are superimposed on consciousness in the spontaneous drama of its own modification). This profound, natural, and native abiding in and as consciousness itself is the final or most basic means for Realizing the Liberating Truth of existence.

THREE

When you directly inspect self and objects in the manner I have just described, all arising conditions (including body, emotions, mind, and the sense of being a defined, separate, and limited self-consciousness) are observed to be mere relations of consciousness. What is more, that consciousness itself, when it is directly located and profoundly identified with, is not found or felt to be separate, limited, individual, or in any sense unhappy. And all of the objects, relations, and states that appear to that consciousness are, from the point of view of consciousness, intuitively felt to be transparent, or merely apparent, unnecessary, and non-binding modifications of itself.

Therefore, the consideration of consciousness (from the point of view of consciousness) eventually, inevitably, spontaneously, and naturally (prior to thought or the knowledge or experience of any object, condition, or state other than itself) Realizes consciousness to be Transcendental Consciousness, or the Ultimate Principle in which egoic consciousness and all experiences are arising. When the

Condition of consciousness is thus Realized, consciousness (as Consciousness) is Obvious as the Divine Condition that is at the root of attention and at the heart of all conscious beings. And, what is more, the objects of consciousness are Realized to be not <u>independent</u> relations of consciousness, but only apparent, unnecessary, and non-binding modifications of That which <u>is</u> Consciousness Itself. That is to say, the phenomenal cosmos is ultimately Realized to be a Mysterious or non-mechanical, spontaneous, and unnecessary (or inherently non-binding) modification of the Subjective Radiance, All-Pervading Energy, or Love-Bliss that is Identical to Consciousness Itself.

FOUR

On the basis of this radical consideration and Realization, it becomes spontaneously Obvious that there is One Principle, which is Radiant Transcendental Being, Consciousness, Love-Bliss, or Eternal Happiness, and not, in Truth or Reality, two Principles—that is, consciousness and everything (or the Substance) that appears to be other than or object to consciousness. Consciousness is the One Self-Evident and Self-Radiant Principle. It is Transcendental Divine Being, Love-Bliss, or Eternal Happiness. And nothing that can arise as experience (or modification) is necessary or binding to It.

What you must Realize or Awaken into (by first acknowledging and consenting to submit to your own native standpoint) is That Self-Evident Radiant Consciousness that is the Real, Transcendental, and Divine Condition of self and not-self. If That is Realized as the Obvious, then there is inherent Freedom—and conditional existence, experience, or attention has no necessity or binding power. That Realization is the Condition and not merely the Goal of existence. And when It is Realized most profoundly, conditional existence becomes as if transparent, or even non-existent—Transfigured and Outshined in the One Transcendental Condition.

III

The
Perfect
Practice

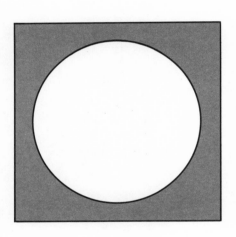

Be Consciousness.

Contemplate Consciousness.

Transcend everything in Consciousness.

This is the Epitome of the Way of Truth.

ONE

Be *consciousness, inherently free in relation to all objects.*

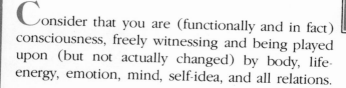

Consider that you are (functionally and in fact) consciousness, freely witnessing and being played upon (but not actually changed) by body, life-energy, emotion, mind, self-idea, and all relations.

Then <u>be</u> consciousness, and function <u>as</u> (or from the position of) consciousness itself—instead of persisting in the conventional and functionally untrue presumption that you are a body-mind (or an always already modified, qualified, limited, defined, and named conditional or psycho-physical entity).

To be and function as (or from the point of view of) consciousness is not itself to Realize what consciousness is (or its ultimate Status), but it is to be in the obvious right or factual attitude or disposition, as consciousness in free relationship to experience.

To be consciousness (<u>related</u> to rather than <u>identical</u> to all that is seeming to be self) is to be free as consciousness itself (rather than a consciousness mechanically bound by a presumption of identity rather than relatedness in the context of the body-mind).

The body-mind is what you call "I."

Consciousness as the body-mind is Narcissus, the separate and separative ego (or self-contraction), identical to experience.

In the state of identification with the body-mind, consciousness is a subject suffering from the absurd presumption that it is identical to its own object.

Consciousness itself is inherently and always prior to experience.

Consciousness is always only related to experience, and, therefore, it is never, as itself, an expression, result, container, servant, or prisoner of experience.

Consciousness is inherently free of the implications or effects of the body-mind and the cosmos of Nature.

Consciousness is not unhappy, afraid, sorrowful, depressed, angry, hungry, lustful, thoughtful, threatened by bodily mortality, or implicated in the alternately pleasurable (or positive) and painful (or negative) states of the body and of Nature.

Consciousness is presently, always, and only related to (or witnessing and seeming to be played upon by) the mechanical or functional states of the body-mind in the realm of Nature.

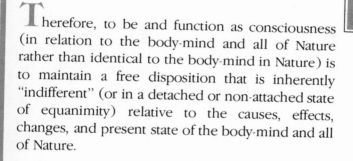

Therefore, to be and function as consciousness (in relation to the body-mind and all of Nature rather than identical to the body-mind in Nature) is to maintain a free disposition that is inherently "indifferent" (or in a detached or non-attached state of equanimity) relative to the causes, effects, changes, and present state of the body-mind and all of Nature.

To be or function as free consciousness in relation to every moment is the "pure" or inherently balanced disposition, and that disposition will inevitably cause or permit the body-mind also to achieve a natural state of equanimity.

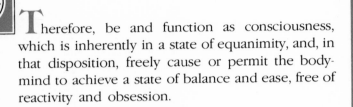

Therefore, be and function as consciousness, which is inherently in a state of equanimity, and, in that disposition, freely cause or permit the body-mind to achieve a state of balance and ease, free of reactivity and obsession.

When this has been done, energy and attention are free of bondage to the "I" of Narcissus, and thus free for the second stage of the Perfect Practice.

TWO

Contemplate or meditate on consciousness itself, prior to all objects, until its Transcendental Condition becomes Obvious.

Enter into the consideration (or deep, profound, and most direct exploration) of consciousness itself, until its Location, Condition, Nature, State, and Status are Realized.

This is a matter of turning attention (which is the functioning consciousness or essence of self) <u>from</u> its objects (in the form of self-idea, mind, emotion, internal life-energy, desire, body, and their relations) and <u>to</u> its Source-Condition.

It is not a matter of inverting upon or meditating on the "I" or egoic self (in the manner of Narcissus).

It is not a matter of worshipping, inverting upon, meditating on, or identifying with the objective (or witnessed) inner self, or essence of egoity.

It is a matter, first of all, of understanding that the essential self is not an entity but the activity of manifest or functional attention.

Consciousness as attention (tending to identify itself with the "I" or body-mind and to contract, via the body-mind, from the threatening field of Nature, or from the Universal Objective Energy that pervades all of Nature) must understand itself (or its own error) and transcend or Realize itself in its own Source-Condition (which is Radiant Transcendental Divine Being, Consciousness, and Happiness, or Love-Bliss).

In appearance, the meditative practice whereby the Condition of consciousness is Realized involves inversion upon the inner self, but it is not in fact a process of inversion upon the conditional and individuated self.

Rather, right meditative inversion is the most direct means for transcending the ego, or the separate and separative self, by turning the essential or basic self-consciousness (or consciousness as attention) to the consideration of That in which attention (and thus the individuated and conditional self-consciousness) is always presently arising.

Therefore, right meditative practice is not a matter of the extroversion of attention toward any object, nor is it a matter of the Narcissistic introversion of attention upon the subjective interior of the body-mind or egoic self.

It is a matter of the yielding (or dissolving) of attention (or self-consciousness itself) into the Source-Condition from which it is presently and always arising.

The practice in its most direct form is a matter of passively allowing attention to settle spontaneously in the primal Feeling of Being, or move naturally into the primal Feeling of Happiness, or even move toward any object it will (or any object that you might choose as a focus of attention) in any moment, but, in the moment of the arising of any "present object" of attention, That to Which (or in Whom) attention, or the "present object," or Happiness is arising should be Noticed and entered into (or Identified with) most profoundly.

This practice is best done by first gazing and then feeling into the region of the right side of the heart (which is the place from which attention first emerges), so that the "present object" that is attention itself (or the most rudimentary self-consciousness and object-consciousness) may be considered there (free of distraction by the outgoing motives of the body-mind), until the primal Feeling of Being or Happiness is Located in the right side of the heart.

Then continue to merge attention in that Happiness, until the Subjective Space of Consciousness, or the Feeling of Being, becomes Obvious beyond the objective heart-focus.

This gazing and feeling is naturally made possible by the submission of attention to the Attractiveness of the Current of Feeling Itself (at Its Root or point of Origin, rather than at any other point in the body).

The bodily Root or Origin of the primary Feeling of Being is Located (or Found) in the right side of the heart as the Feeling of profound, constant, original, uncaused, and unqualified Happiness (or Love-Bliss).

That Current of Happiness is Transmitted, Revealed, Intensified, and made Attractive by Grace in the Company of the Adept Spiritual Master.

Gradually, this practice becomes profound Identification with Being or Consciousness Itself, prior to individuation as a self, prior to any objective referents, and prior to the primary sense of relatedness, so that Its State and Status are Obvious as Transcendental Being and Eternal Love-Bliss, or Self-Radiant Happiness.

THREE

Abide as Transcendental Consciousness, inherently transcending but not strategically excluding or seeking any or all objects, and thus tacitly recognize all objects in and as Radiant Transcendental Being, Consciousness, Love-Bliss, or Happiness, until all objects are Outshined in That.

Consciousness, or Being Itself, is Transcendental, or prior to attention in the cosmic or conditional realm of Nature.

Transcendental Consciousness is Reality, or the Source-Condition of attention, self, body-mind, and all of Nature (including the universal or all-pervading and apparently Objective Energy of which all the objects, conditions, states, or manifest individuals in Nature are composed).

When Transcendental Consciousness, or the simple Feeling of Being, is Awakened as the Real "I" or Self, the Indefinable Identity of consciousness, or the Infinite Source-Condition of attention, then the ego-"I," or self-contraction, or self-possessed body-mind is transcended, and the Condition of Nature is Obvious, even in the moment of spontaneous attention to the conditions and relations of the body-mind.

Such Obviousness is the primary characteristic of the Awakening to the ultimate or Enlightened stage of life, and only that Awakening manifests as the capability for fulfilling and completing the third stage of the Perfect Practice, which is the ultimate and radical form of the Way that I Teach.

Therefore, when Identification with the Transcendental Divine Consciousness, or Feeling of Being, is complete (tacit, uncaused, and undisturbed), simply Abide as That and allow all conditions (or all of Nature) to arise or not arise in the Self-Radiance and Subjective Space of Transcendental Being.

As conditions arise in That "open-eyed" or Radiant Consciousness, they are recognized (and inherently transcended) as transparent, or merely apparent, unnecessary, and non-binding modifications of That.

Abiding and recognizing thus, let actions arise spontaneously in and via the inherent Love-Bliss of Radiant Transcendental Being, until all conditions (of self and/or not-self) are Transfigured, Transformed, and then Translated (or Outshined) in the Radiant Transcendental Being (Who is the heart, the Divine Condition, and the Free Domain of all beings).

This Perfect Practice is the Epitome of the consideration and practice of the Way that I Teach. It is the basis on which all of the philosophy and every discipline associated with this Way are developed and fulfilled. Therefore, this book is the Epitome of all that I am here to say to you about the Realization of Truth and Happiness.

IV

Freedom

The conventions of human life and civilization are based on the mechanical, arbitrary, and uninspected identification of consciousness with the patterns of experience. Thus, human pursuits are, as a matter of convention and habit, dedicated toward self-centered elaboration of experience, self-fulfillment via experience, and escape in (or from) the context of experience. Both science and religion are conventions of egoity in the embrace and pursuit and avoidance of experience. All conventional human pursuits are a bewildered search founded on uninspected egoic identification with experience rather than radically intuitive Identification with the Happiness of Transcendental Consciousness, or Being Itself. Thus, either experience, or Objective Nature, or materiality, or God as the Reality that is Other than self and Nature tends to be presumed and propagandized as the First, the Ultimate, the One, or the Most Important Principle—but such presumptions are simply the ultimate Illusions or deluded Visions that are developed from the base of the ego (or Consciousness limited by experiencing).

If you are free to be supremely intelligent and devoted to Truth and Happiness, then the Way is most direct and profound Identification with Consciousness, or the Feeling of Being, prior to all doubt, prior to any limitation by experience, prior to all "looking" at objects, within or without, high or low, positive or negative, and prior to any qualification by the sense of relatedness. When this Identification is complete, so that it is not dependent on any act or state of attention, or mind, or emotion, or desire, or life-energy, or body, or Nature itself, then all experience, or the total realm of Nature and egoity, is inherently and tacitly recognized in That (or as a transparent, unnecessary, and non-binding modification of Radiant Transcendental Being). When this Enlightened disposition is Awake, the Way is simply to Abide in and as that Radiant Condition of Being, inherently transcending all conditions—but recognizing and allowing them rather than resisting and excluding them. And persistence in this Radiant Identity and recognition Transfigures, Transforms, and ultimately Outshines the body-mind and all worlds. In the meantime there is simple Abiding in and as the Radiant Love-Bliss of Transcendental Being—and such Abiding spontaneously expresses Itself as Radiance, Happiness, Blessing, and Help in all relations.

TWO

The Ultimate Wisdom inherently understands, transcends, and stands free of the life-drama. Happiness, Transcendental Consciousness, or Being Itself inherently transcends the confrontation between the ego and Nature.

Every ego-"I," or self-possessed body-mind, is involved in a passionate and mortal struggle with the Force and the forces and the parts of Objective Nature.

Every ego-"I" is active as the opponent of all opponents, but there is no final victory—and every opposition is an irrational (or fruitless) search for equanimity, peace, and love.

Every ego-"I" always tends to desire and seek a perfect refuge from irrational opponents. That strategy of self-preservation is entertained in temporary pleasures and solitary places, but it is not finally attained. Only the ego-"I," the separate and separative body-mind, is opposed and opposing—and every opposition is an irrational (or fruitless) search for freedom.

The ego-"I" is inherently, always, and irrationally (or meaninglessly) opposed. The "other" is always an opponent (in effect, if not by intention). The ego-"I" is confronted only by binding forces, and it is itself a force that is tending to bind every "other." The "other" and the ego-"I" are mad relations, always together in the growling pit, bound by Nature to do Nature's deeds to one another. And as experience increases, it begins to become clear that Nature itself is an Immense Pattern that always seeks and inevitably attains superiority, dominance, and destruction of every part and self.

Therefore, the Great Other—whether It is called Nature or Nature's God—is your Opponent, not your Refuge. And the very perception and conception of difference (or Otherness) is the Sign that the ego-"I," rather than Truth, is the presumed basis of conscious existence.

Truth is <u>prior</u> or eternal Freedom and Humor, whether or not the Other or the Opponent seems to be present. Therefore, Truth is the only Refuge. And if you surrender to the Truth, which is Transcendental Being, Consciousness, or Happiness (the Subjective Source of self and all that is objective and Objective to it), then there is an Awakening from this nightmare of condemned life and its passionate search for pleasure, victory, and escape.

When the response or Awakening to Truth is Real, then the frightened and self-bound motive toward the world (and the inevitable round of pleasures, confrontations, doubts, searches, and always temporary releases) begins to fall away. The mortal self becomes simpler in action, more free of habitual reactions to insult and frustration of purpose, more humorous in the face of Nature and all the fools of Nature, more compassionate, and inclined to selfless (or sorrowless) love. The ego-"I" that is Awakened beyond itself is inclined to set others free of itself, rather than to bind them to itself, or to themselves, or to one another. The ego-"I" that is nearly dissolved is more often solitary, more deeply renounced, without cares or motivations or doubts or angry despair of self or others, but firmly Absorbed in Transcendental Being. At last, all of this rising of self and world is recognized to be an unnecessary and superficial dream, a stressful inclination that is gradually forgotten or suddenly Outshined in the prior Happiness of Divine Existence.

The usable Lesson of a difficult life proves that you must observe, understand, and transcend your own conditional personality and destiny. Every individual is only seeking not to be destroyed. Therefore, understand and become more tolerant of others. Cease to struggle with others and yourself. Do not become bound up in the usual search for dominance, consolation, pleasure, and release. There is neither Final Release nor Ultimate Happiness in the objective or the subjective realms of merely conditional consciousness.

Observe and understand the theatre of "I." Learn to be free of the reactivity and seeking that characterize the self-principle (which is only the body-mind in confrontation with the realm of Nature). Thus, allow attention to be free of the motive toward the body-mind and its relations. Let attention be free instead to transcend this world-theatre and to Abide in the Transcendental Domain that is at the Origin of conditional consciousness. Then, if the body-mind and all of Nature arise, see all of it from the Original Position of Transcendental Consciousness. See that self and Nature are an unnecessary and non-binding Play upon the Radiance or Free Energy of Consciousness or Being Itself.

THREE

Consider all of this, and, by every means of consideration and practice, relax attention from the dilemma and the search associated with the body-mind, high or low in the realm of Nature. In the manner of the first stage of the Perfect Practice, identify with consciousness in daily life and meditation, until the body-mind accepts the discipline of equanimity. When attention is truly free or "indifferent" relative to the motives and states of the body-mind, the second stage of the Perfect Practice can begin.

In the second stage of the Perfect Practice, yield attention to the Feeling-Space in the right side of the heart. Consider or feel every "present object" there. Then transcend attention, the present object, and the objective space of the heart by Feeling Being, or directly intuiting the Subjective Space that is Consciousness Itself, prior to psycho-physical self-consciousness.

Do not merely <u>look</u> at the root of attention in the heart. The root that is thus "seen" is merely another <u>object</u> of attention. Rather, Locate the root of attention (or the Root-Location of Happiness) in the heart via the Current of Feeling, and then intuit and Be Consciousness there, prior to any object. Be Consciousness, Happiness, or Being Itself, prior to objects, until Its Status becomes Obvious, beyond any possibility of doubt.

The purpose of going to the right side of the heart (in the second stage of the Perfect Practice) is to establish attention in its <u>subjective</u> root. The Locus that is Revealed in the right side of the heart is the bodily <u>root</u> of attention (or the bodily gateway to the Source of mind, which Source is unqualified Happiness). The brain, the abdominal region, and every other extended part of the body, including the middle and the left side of the heart, are merely bodily <u>objects</u> of attention (or extensions of mind or life-energy at a distance from the heart-root), and mere attention to any one of them is itself an involvement in a motion of mind or life-energy that leads to all kinds of gross and subtle objects. Therefore, when attention is stably free for the second stage of the Perfect Practice, constantly Locate the Current of primal Happiness, or the Feeling of Being, in the right side of the heart. Do not merely <u>look</u> at the objective heart-root, but <u>feel</u> at the heart-root, and from the heart-root in relation to any or every object that may arise to the attention there. Transcend every object in the Transcendental Subject (or Consciousness) by Feeling as the Being or Primal Happiness in the right side of the heart. Feel as the Being (or as Happiness), and then meditate on the Being that is Consciousness (or Aware as fundamental Happiness), until it becomes clear that Consciousness, or Happiness, or Being Itself has no objects, or knowledge, or limitations at all. Then, when objects return, feel and tacitly recognize them as projections in That Radiant Space that is Wholly and Transcendentally Subjective, Rooted in Being, or Only Consciousness.

In the third stage of the Perfect Practice, the countless objects of conditional Nature are cognized and recognized in the Space of Consciousness, or Being Itself, but there is no loss of Transcendental or Divine Self-Consciousness, prior Freedom, and Happiness.

FOUR

Be Consciousness.

This stage is complete when the body-mind is in a stable state of equanimity (or "indifference") and attention is free to fall back into Consciousness Itself.

Contemplate Consciousness.

This stage is complete when there is no longer the slightest feeling or possibility of doubt relative to the Status of Consciousness as the Transcendental and Subjective Source of self and all of Nature.

Transcend everything in Consciousness.

This stage is complete when there is no longer any arising of attention to any form of self or world, but all Objectified existence is utterly Outshined in Subjective or Transcendental Existence.

Accept the Freedom and Happiness that is inherent in Existence Itself.

FIVE

Be Conscious as the Feeling of Being
and Realize that It <u>Is</u> Radiant Happiness,
or Freedom Itself.
Consciousness Is Radiant Being.
Freedom Is Inherent Happiness,
or Love,
not self-contraction.
Love Is Recognition of the world
in the Radiance of Being,
until the world is Outshined.

This is the Word of Da Eleutherios,
the Eternal One,
Who is Ever-Free,
Whose Mere Existence Liberates all beings,
Freely, Liberally, Gracefully,
and Without Ceasing.

ΕΛΕΥΘΕΡΙΟΣ

An
Invitation
to Practice

ONE

Anciently, the spiritual trial of ego-transcending or self-transcending practice was considered the most creative and praiseworthy endeavor a human being could undertake. *The Liberator (Eleutherios)* calls men and women in our time to hear the Teaching of the Spiritual Master and to take up the radical practice of self-transcendence.

Practitioners of the Way study and adapt to natural disciplines which establish the body-mind in a state of non-attachment, equanimity, and ease. The purpose of these disciplines is simply to free energy and attention for the unique meditative processes that ultimately become the Perfect Practice described in this book. Thus, from the very beginning the essence of practice is the consideration of, meditation on, and Realization of Consciousness, the Liberating Truth.

The following essay written by Master Da Free John offers his ultimate recommendation to anyone who responds to his Teaching.

What do I recommend? I recommend the most direct and, ultimately, radical Way. Therefore, I recommend the "Perfect Practice." But I have also seen that people do not tend to maintain the Awakened point of view of this Practice, even though they grasp and sympathize with my Argument to a significant degree. Therefore, I have proposed a "yoga of consideration," a practical culture of self-transcending (and attention-liberating) insight and self-surrender, as the means of preparation for the fullest Realization of the third or radical stage of the Perfect Practice.

The first stage of the Perfect Practice may be done directly, exactly in the form I have described, by a very few. Such individuals immediately and permanently *"hear"* and *"see"* the Spiritual Master, and so they become spontaneously self-renounced (or free for profound practice), and they progress quickly, from the first to the second and then to the third or radical stage of this Perfect Practice, by Grace in the Company (or via the Transmission) of the Spiritual Master.

However, most individuals are habitually and profoundly bound and unconsciously controlled by their identification and struggle with self, mind, emotion, life-energies, desires, body, and all kinds of conditional relations. Their necessary first course of practice (whereby the first and second stages of the Perfect Practice are fulfilled via a number of effective disciplines) is described in the general and esoteric Teachings of the *"Way of Insight"* and the *"Way of Faith."*

Everyone is invited to directly consider this book, and all of the other examples of the radical Argument, but each one should also really practice, and that means that each one must begin as a beginner and proceed gradually, but surely and directly, toward qualification for practice of the Way in its most radical or priorly Enlightened form. When the body-mind has become stabilized *in equanimity, when energy and attention are thus free of the binding power of experience and the motives of the egoic pattern of life, and when the Transcendental Consciousness or Happiness beyond self-consciousness and other-consciousness (or object-consciousness) is Realized as the Obvious (beyond even the most subtle feeling of doubt), then there can be instruction and practice in the special disciplines associated with the third or radical stage of the Perfect Practice.*

TWO

Master Da Free John's practical Teaching embraces three forms of approach to Transcendental Realization. These three are the Perfect Practice, the Way of Insight, and the Way of Faith. All three approaches are based upon the Teaching and the Perfect Practice described in this book. Either the Way of Insight or the Way of Faith is likely to be the form of approach for which most people are immediately qualified. Each of the three "schools" contains a complete preparatory culture, whereby the first two stages of the Perfect Practice may be truly fulfilled, but actual fulfillment of the practice of any one of the three approaches requires a sincere interest and a dedicated response to the Teaching, the Spiritual Master, and the possibility of finally taking up the ultimate or third stage of the Perfect Practice described in this book. All three approaches are based on the attitude of self-transcendence, surrender, and understanding of the

Teaching, and each of the schools involves specific practices and disciplines which prepare the individual for the ultimate intuitive Realization of Truth.

The Perfect Practice itself is for the unusually qualified individual, who demonstrates the unique qualities of equanimity and free attention during an initial period of study, meditation, and practice of the Teaching and its foundation disciplines. The Way of Insight is for the person who is especially gifted with the capacity to grow by observing and understanding and transcending the self through discriminative intelligence. And the Way of Faith is specifically intended for the practitioner in whom the naturally self-transcending disposition of devotion and feeling-surrender is dominant.

The meditative practices and life-disciplines of these three Ways, as well as the descriptions of the stages and signs of spiritual maturity, are treated by Master Da in his numerous works. The practical literature covers a wide range of important topics—from diet, exercise, and sexuality to devotional culture, the moral discipline of service, and the significance of community life. The essential literature consists of Master Da's critical argument about politics, science, religion, and esotericism; his specific technical instructions on the practice of the Way that he Teaches; and his confessional descriptions of the Great Realization. Together these profound volumes form a unique treasury of practical and spiritual wisdom.

To readers of this book wishing to know more about Master Da's Teaching we recommend, as a first step, the following publications: *The Knee of Listening* (Master Da's spiritual autobiography), *The Method of the Siddhas, Scientific Proof of the Existence of God Will Soon Be Announced by the White House!,* and *The Enlightenment of the Whole Body.*

THREE

The spiritual fellowship of practitioners of the Way Taught by Master Da Free John is called THE JOHANNINE DAIST COMMUNION. "Johannine" means "having the character of John," which means "one through whom God is Gracious." "Da" is a Name of the Living, Eternal, Infinite, and Graceful Divine Being or Reality. When used to refer to the Spiritual Master, "Da" is a Title of respect and an indication of spiritual stature and function, meaning "one who Gives or Transmits the Divine Influence and Awakening to living beings."

The Communion has five divisions:

THE LAUGHING MAN INSTITUTE, which is the public education division.

THE FREE COMMUNION CHURCH, which is the devotional Culture of Celebration for practicing students.

THE CRAZY WISDOM FELLOWSHIP, which is the educational and cultural organization for maturing practitioners.

THE ADVAITAYANA BUDDHIST ORDER, which is reserved for the advanced or esoteric stages of practice.

THE FREE RENUNCIATE ORDER, which consists of devotees who have Realized the ultimate stage of practice of the Way.

If you feel moved to take up the Way, or if you would like more information about the Teaching, our publications, or the programs of study we offer to the public as well as to practicing students, you are cordially invited to contact us at the address below:

The Laughing Man Institute
P.O. Box 3680
Clearlake, California 95422

ELEUTHERIOS

THE ELEUTHERIAN MISSION

This book is made available to you by the Eleutherian Mission. Our purpose is to disseminate *The Liberator (Eleutherios)* throughout the world and to offer spiritual service to anyone anywhere who responds to its message.

Liberation while alive has been the promise of all great Teachers and the urgent dream of all mankind. *The Liberator (Eleutherios)* describes the Truth that sets us free, and constitutes an invitation to everyone who would lead a truly liberated life.

You may help the Eleutherian Mission in the following ways:

by patronizing the worldwide publication and promotion of this book

by assisting us to arrange worldwide presentations and lectures on the Teaching of *The Liberator (Eleutherios)*

by cooperating with us to translate the book into all languages

If you would like to know more about the Mission's work and about other books by Da Free John, or if you wish to help, through your patronage, the spreading of this great Teaching, please write:

The Eleutherian Mission
P.O. Box 3680
Clearlake, California 95422

THE BOOKS OF MASTER DA FREE JOHN

SOURCE TEXTS

THE KNEE OF LISTENING
The Early Life and Radical Spiritual Teachings of
Bubba [Da] Free John
$6.95 paper

THE METHOD OF THE SIDDHAS
Talks with Bubba [Da] Free John on the Spiritual Technique
of the Saviors of Mankind
$12.95 paper

THE HYMN OF THE MASTER
A Confessional Recitation on the Mystery of the Spiritual
Master based on the principal verses of the Guru Gita *(freely*
selected, rendered, and adapted)
$8.95 paper

THE FOUR FUNDAMENTAL QUESTIONS
Talks and essays about human experience and the actual
practice of an Enlightened Way of Life
$1.95 paper

THE LIBERATOR (ELEUTHERIOS)
A summation of the "radical process" of Enlightenment, or
God-Realization, taught by the "Western Adept," Master Da
Free John
$12.95 cloth, $6.95 paper

THE ENLIGHTENMENT OF THE WHOLE BODY
A Rational and New Prophetic Revelation of the Truth of Religion, Esoteric Spirituality, and the Divine Destiny of Man
$18.95 paper

SCIENTIFIC PROOF OF THE EXISTENCE OF GOD WILL SOON BE ANNOUNCED BY THE WHITE HOUSE!
Prophetic Wisdom about the Myths and Idols of mass culture and popular religious cultism, the new priesthood of scientific and political materialism, and the secrets of Enlightenment hidden in the body of Man
$12.95 paper

THE PARADOX OF INSTRUCTION
An Introduction to the Esoteric Spiritual Teaching of Bubba [Da] Free John
$12.95 paper

NIRVANASARA
Radical Transcendentalism and the Introduction of Advaitayana Buddhism
$9.95 paper

MANUALS OF PRACTICE

COMPULSORY DANCING
Talks and Essays on the spiritual and evolutionary necessity of emotional surrender to the Life-Principle
$2.95 paper

THE WAY THAT I TEACH
Talks on the Intuition of Eternal Life
$12.95 paper

THE YOGA OF CONSIDERATION AND
THE WAY THAT I TEACH
*Talks and essays on the distinction between preliminary
practices and the radical Way of prior Enlightenment*
$8.95 paper

BODILY WORSHIP OF THE LIVING GOD
The Esoteric Practice of Prayer Taught by Da Free John
$12.95 paper

THE BODILY SACRIFICE OF ATTENTION
*Introductory Talks on Radical Understanding and the Life of
Divine Ignorance*
$12.95 paper

"I" IS THE BODY OF LIFE
*Talks and Essays on the Art and Science of Equanimity and
the Self-Transcending Process of Radical Understanding*
$12.95 paper

THE BODILY LOCATION OF HAPPINESS
*On the Incarnation of the Divine Person and the
Transmission of Love-Bliss*
$8.95 paper

PRACTICAL TEXTS

CONSCIOUS EXERCISE AND THE TRANSCENDENTAL SUN
The principle of love applied to exercise and the method of common physical action. A science of whole body wisdom, or true emotion, intended most especially for those engaged in religious or spiritual life
$12.95 cloth

THE EATING GORILLA COMES IN PEACE
The Transcendental Principle of Life Applied to Diet and the Regenerative Discipline of True Health
$18.95 paper

RAW GORILLA
The Principles of Regenerative Raw Diet Applied in True Spiritual Practice
$3.95 paper

LOVE OF THE TWO-ARMED FORM
The Free and Regenerative Function of Sexuality in Ordinary Life, and the Transcendence of Sexuality in True Religious or Spiritual Practice
$18.95 paper

For Children

WHAT TO REMEMBER TO BE HAPPY
A Spiritual Way of Life for Your First Fourteen Years or So
$3.95 paper

I AM HAPPINESS
A Rendering for Children of the Spiritual Adventure of
Master Da Free John
Adapted by Daji Bodha and Lynne Closser from
The Knee of Listening *by Master Da Free John*
$9.95 paper

Periodicals

CRAZY WISDOM
The Monthly Journal of The Crazy Wisdom Fellowship
12 copies $25.00

THE LAUGHING MAN
The Alternative to Scientific Materialism and Religious
Provincialism
4 copies (quarterly) $10.00

The books of Da Free John are available from fine bookstores
or by mail order from The Dawn Horse Book Depot. To order
by mail, please add to price shown postage and handling of
$1.25 for first book, $.35 for each additional book. California
residents add 6% sales tax. Address to:

THE DAWN HORSE BOOK DEPOT
P.O. Box 3680, Dept. L
Clearlake, CA 95422

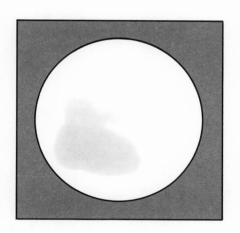